From My Heart to Yours
Copyright 2000 by Zondervan
ISBN 0-310-98437-8

Requests for information should be addressed to:

Inspirio, the gift group of Zondervan
Grand Rapids, Michigan 49530
http://www.inspiriogifts.com

Compiler: Emily Klotz
Project Manager: Patricia Matthews
Associate Editor: Molly C. Detweiler
Photos: Photographic Concepts
Design: Pam Thomson/Mark Veldheer
Printed in China

02 03/HK/4 3 2

From My
Heart to
Yours

inspirio

May the Lord make your love increase and overflow for each other and for everyone else.

1 Thessalonians 3:12

Some people come into our
lives and quickly go.
Some stay for awhile
and leave footprints
on our hearts.
And we are never,
ever the same.

The LORD your God is with you, he is mighty to save. He will take great delight in you, he will quiet you with his love, he will rejoice over you with singing.

Zephaniah 3:17

The most important trip you
may take in life
is meeting people halfway.

Henry Boye

God is able to make all grace
abound to you, so that in all
things at all times, having all
that you need, you will
abound in every good work.

2 Corinthians 9:8

Sometimes in life, you find a special friend, Someone who changes your life just by being there, Someone who makes you believe, That there is really good in the world.

May the God who gives endurance and encouragement give you a spirit of
unity among yourselves as
you follow Christ Jesus.

Romans 15:5

Love one another deeply,
from the heart.

1 Peter 1:22

Keep thy friend
Under thy own life's key.

William Shakespeare

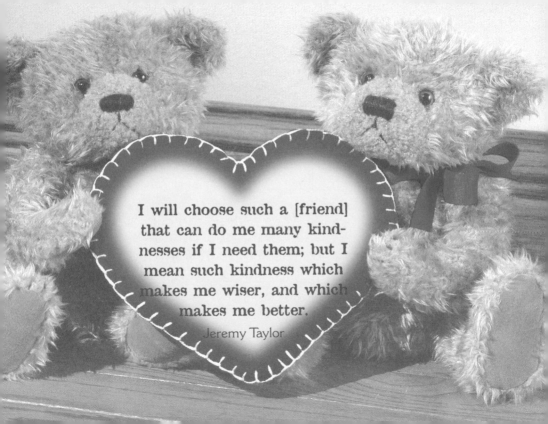

I will choose such a [friend]
that can do me many kind-
nesses if I need them; but I
mean such kindness which
makes me wiser, and which
makes me better.

Jeremy Taylor

My heart leaps for joy
and I will give thanks
to the LORD in song.

Psalm 28:7

The heart has
reasons that reason
does not understand.

May the Lord direct your hearts into God's love and Christ's perseverance.

2 Thessalonians 3:5

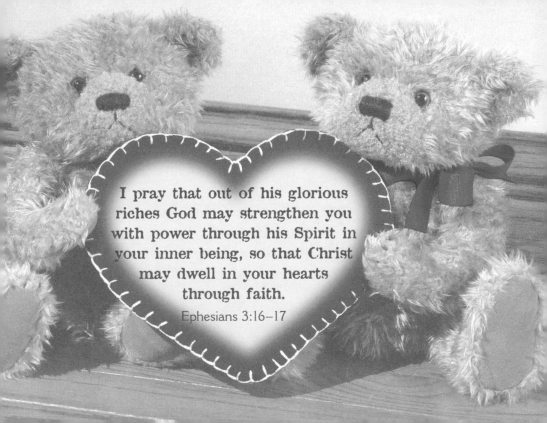

I pray that out of his glorious riches God may strengthen you with power through his Spirit in your inner being, so that Christ may dwell in your hearts through faith.

Ephesians 3:16–17

What we have once enjoyed
we can never lose.
All that we love deeply
becomes a part of us.

Helen Keller

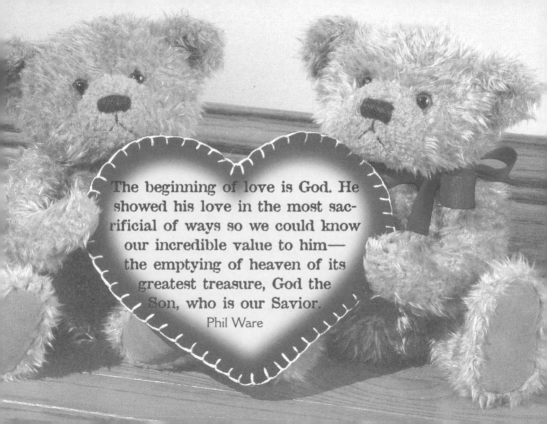

The beginning of love is God. He showed his love in the most sacrificial of ways so we could know our incredible value to him— the emptying of heaven of its greatest treasure, God the Son, who is our Savior.

Phil Ware

We know that in all things
God works for the good of
those who love him, who
have been called according to
his purpose.

Romans 8:28

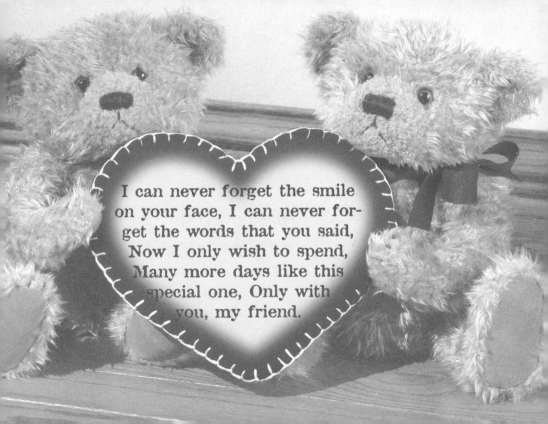

I can never forget the smile
on your face, I can never forget the words that you said,
Now I only wish to spend,
Many more days like this
special one, Only with
you, my friend.

O Friendship, flavor
of flowers! O lively
sprite of life!

Grimoald

What sunshine is to flowers, smiles are to humanity.

Addison

A friend is someone who can
make you laugh
when you think you'll never
smile again.

If I had a star for every
time you made me smile...
I'd have the sky in my hands.

A smooth and steadfast mind,
Gentle thoughts and
calm desires,
Hearts with equal love com-
bined, Kindle never-dying
fires.

Thomas Carew

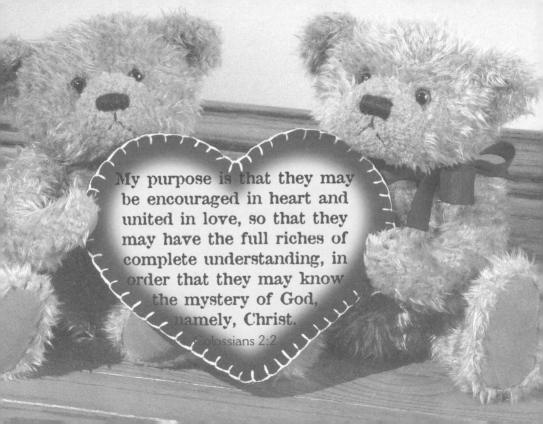

My purpose is that they may be encouraged in heart and united in love, so that they may have the full riches of complete understanding, in order that they may know the mystery of God, namely, Christ.

Colossians 2:2

We go on long walks,
And have deep and
meaningful talks.
She is ever and always
my best friend
And I will love her till
the end.

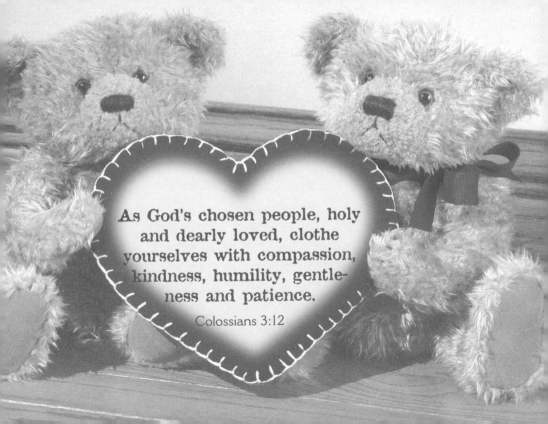

As God's chosen people, holy and dearly loved, clothe yourselves with compassion, kindness, humility, gentleness and patience.

Colossians 3:12

Happiness is a warm cup of tea, a light flaky pastry and a lazy Saturday morning ... all shared with a friend!

May God be gracious to us
and bless us
and make his face shine
upon us.

Psalm 67:1

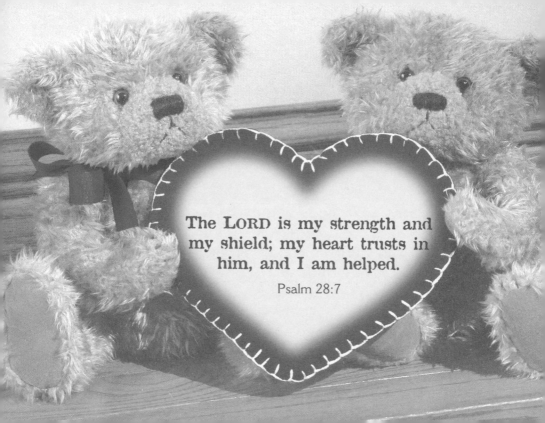

The LORD is my strength and my shield; my heart trusts in him, and I am helped.

Psalm 28:7

The sun, the stars and the
moon above
Are not as wonderful as a
friend's kind love.

Love knows no reasons,
love knows no lies.
Love defies all reasons,
love has no eyes.
But love is not blind,
love sees but doesn't mind.

Speak to one another with psalms, hymns and spiritual songs. Sing and make music in your heart to the Lord, always giving thanks to God the Father for everything.

Ephesians 5:19–20

Kindness in words creates
confidence.
Kindness in thinking creates
profoundness.
Kindness in giving creates
love.

You are my friend, you whom
I love and long for, my joy
and crown!

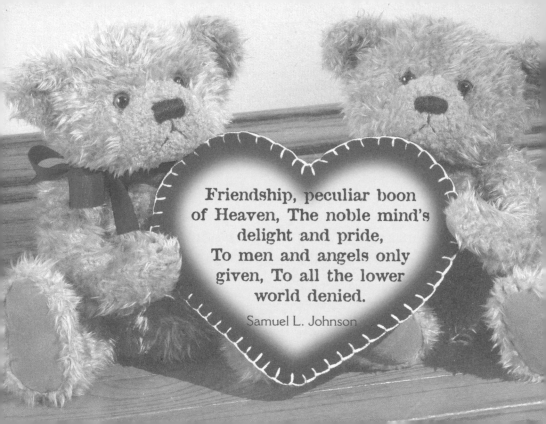

Friendship, peculiar boon of Heaven, The noble mind's delight and pride, To men and angels only given, To all the lower world denied.

Samuel L. Johnson

Every good and perfect gift is from above, coming down from the Father of the heavenly lights, who does not change like shifting shadows.

James 1:17

Because you are my friend, I
am full of joy.
Joy, remain.

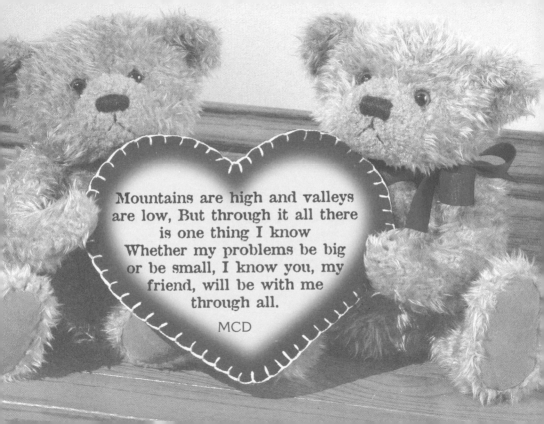

Mountains are high and valleys are low, But through it all there is one thing I know Whether my problems be big or be small, I know you, my friend, will be with me through all.

MCD

There are many things in life
That will catch your eye,
But only a few will catch
your heart...
Pursue those.

A smile is the light in your window that tells others that there is a caring, sharing person inside.

Denis Waitley

We will share with you what-
ever good things the LORD
gives us.

Numbers 10:32

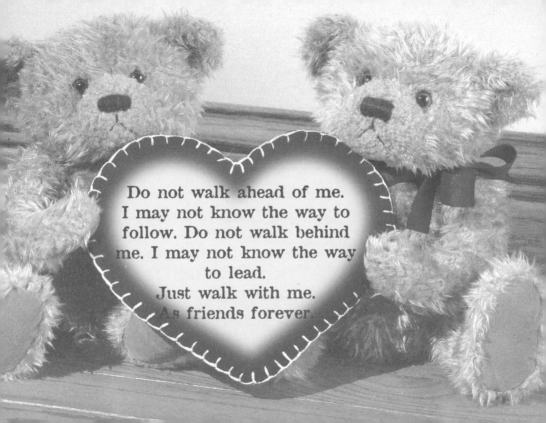

Do not walk ahead of me.
I may not know the way to
follow. Do not walk behind
me. I may not know the way
to lead.
Just walk with me.
As friends forever.

There shall be showers of blessing: This is the promise of love; There shall be seasons refreshing, Sent from the Savior above.

Daniel Webster Whittle

Your love has given me great joy and encouragement.

Philemon 1:7

You gave me life and
showed me kindness,
and in your providence
watched over my spirit,
O Lord.

Job 10:12

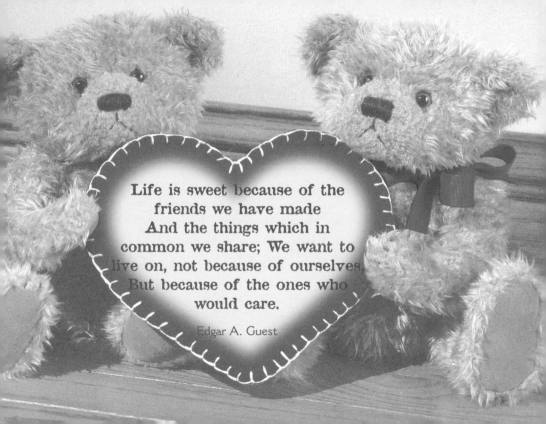

Life is sweet because of the
friends we have made
And the things which in
common we share; We want to
live on, not because of ourselves,
But because of the ones who
would care.

Edgar A. Guest

"I have loved you with an everlasting love;
I have drawn you with loving-kindness," says the Lord.

Jeremiah 31:3

Joy is a net of love that captures souls.

Mother Teresa

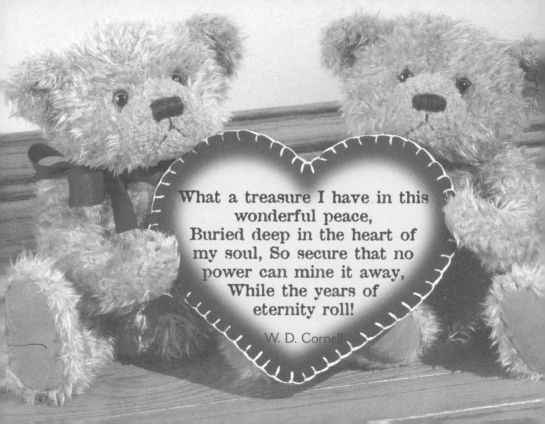

What a treasure I have in this wonderful peace, Buried deep in the heart of my soul, So secure that no power can mine it away, While the years of eternity roll!

W. D. Cornell

Let him who boasts boast about this: that he understands and knows me, that I am the LORD, who exercises kindness, justice and righteousness on earth, for in these I delight.

Jeremiah 9:24

Precious things are very few
in this world.
That is the reason there is
just one you.

I would be friends with you
and have your love.

William Shakespeare

"I led my people with cords
of human kindness,
with ties of love," says the
Lord.

Hosea 11:4

Lord, keep my friend in your arms as I keep her in my prayers. Send sunshine her way today and lift her up. Amen.

From homes of quiet peace
We lift up hands of prayer,
And those Thou gavest
us to love
Commend, Lord, to
Thy care.

William Henry Draper

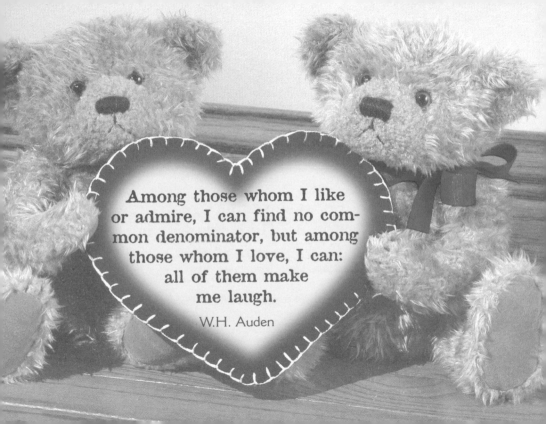

Among those whom I like or admire, I can find no common denominator, but among those whom I love, I can: all of them make me laugh.

W.H. Auden

Because of his great love
for us, God, who is rich
in mercy, made us alive
with Christ.

Ephesians 2:4–5

The fruit of the Spirit is love, joy, peace, patience, kindness, goodness, faithfulness, gentleness and self-control.

Galatians 5:22–23

Friends are kisses blown to
us by angels.

Though one may be overpowered, two can defend themselves. A cord of three strands is not quickly broken.

Ecclesiastes 4:12

Keep me as the apple of your eye, O Lord;
hide me in the shadow of your wings.

Psalm 17:8

A smile is a curve that sets things straight.

We always thank God, the Father of our Lord Jesus Christ, when we pray for you.

Colossians 1:3

It is the things in common
that make relationships
enjoyable,
but it is the little
differences that make
them interesting.

Todd Ruthman

How good and pleasant it is when brothers live together in unity!

Psalm 133:1

Best Friends ...
Love you even when you're
being irrational. Let you take
a bite of their dessert.
Make you laugh when
you're crying. Make life
happier and a lot
more fun!

Try to remember to forget
Anger, worry and regret.
Live while you have
life to live.
Love while you have
love to give.

Spread love everywhere you go: first of all in your own home. Give love to your children, to a wife or husband, to a next-door neighbor.

Mother Teresa

Grace and peace be yours
in abundance through the
knowledge of God and of
Jesus our Lord.

2 Peter 1:2

All of the beautiful senti-
ments in the world
weigh less than a single
lovely action.

James Russell Lowell

Dear friends, since God so loved us, we also ought to love one another.

1 John 4:11

One thing God has spoken,
two things have I heard:
that you, O God, are
strong, and that you,
O Lord, are loving.

Psalm 62:11–12

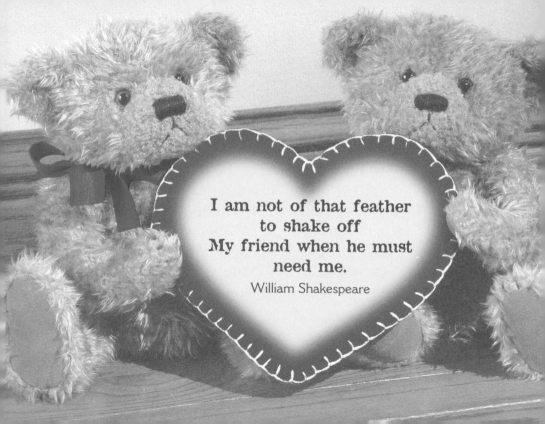

I am not of that feather
to shake off
My friend when he must
need me.

William Shakespeare

To the world you may
be one person,
but to one person you
may be the world.

A friend is someone we turn to when our spirits need a lift, A friend is someone we treasure for our friendship is a gift.

Jean Kyler McManus

The best and most beautiful things in this world cannot be seen or even touched. They must be felt with the heart.

Helen Keller

When it comes to giving love, the opportunities are unlimited, and we are all gifted.

Leo Buscaglia

A friend loves at
all times.

Proverbs 17:17

Perfume and incense bring joy to the heart, and the pleasantness of one's friend springs from his earnest counsel.

Proverbs 27:9

Love puts the fun in together,
The sad in apart,
The hope in tomorrow,
The joy in the heart.

To desire the same things and to reject the same things, constitutes true friendship.

From the fullness of God's grace we have all received one blessing after another.

John 1:16

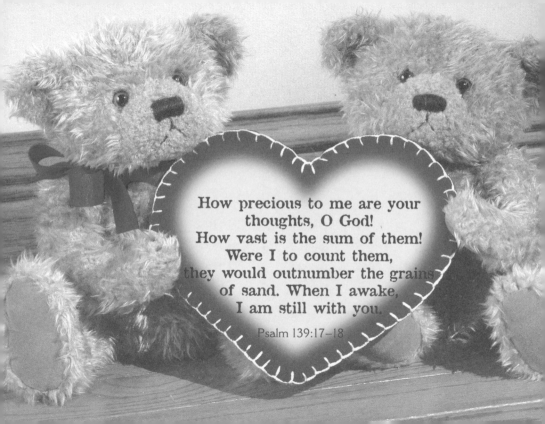

How precious to me are your
thoughts, O God!
How vast is the sum of them!
Were I to count them,
they would outnumber the grains
of sand. When I awake,
I am still with you.

Psalm 139:17–18

The LORD is faithful to all
his promises
and loving toward all
he has made.

Psalm 145:13

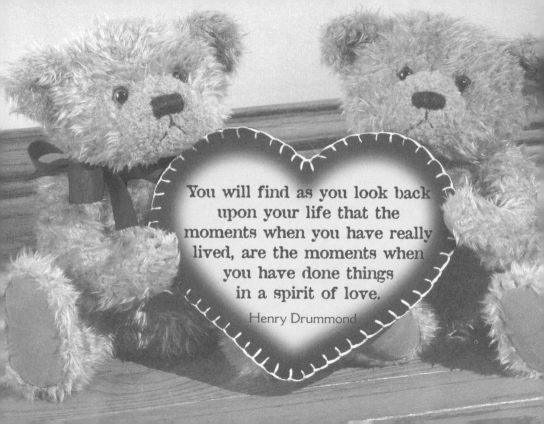

You will find as you look back upon your life that the moments when you have really lived, are the moments when you have done things in a spirit of love.

Henry Drummond

"My unfailing love for you will not be shaken nor my covenant of peace be removed," says the LORD, who has compassion on you.

Isaiah 54:10

God is love. Whoever lives in love lives in God, and God in him.

1 John 4:16

Upon your heart like
paper white,
Let none but friends
presume to write;
And may each line with
friendship given
Direct the sender's
thoughts to Heaven.

Love is not two people gazing
at each other,
but two people looking in the
same direction.

Greater love has no one than this, that he lay down his life for his friends.

John 15:13

Love never fails.

1 Corinthians 13:8

There's a special kind of freedom friends enjoy. Freedom to share innermost thoughts, to show their true feelings. The freedom to simply be themselves.

Keep on loving each other.

Hebrews 13:1

May the LORD, the Maker of
heaven and earth,
bless you from Zion.

Psalm 134:3

Sweet is the scene where
genial friendship plays
The pleasing game of inter-
changing praise.

Oliver Wendell Holmes

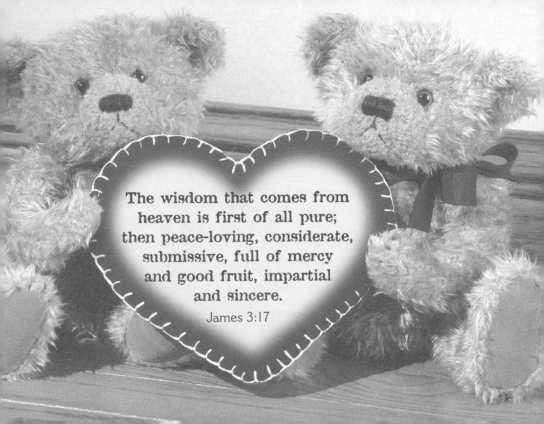

The wisdom that comes from heaven is first of all pure; then peace-loving, considerate, submissive, full of mercy and good fruit, impartial and sincere.

James 3:17

All love that has not friendship for its base, is like a
mansion built upon the sand.

Ella Wheeler Wilcox

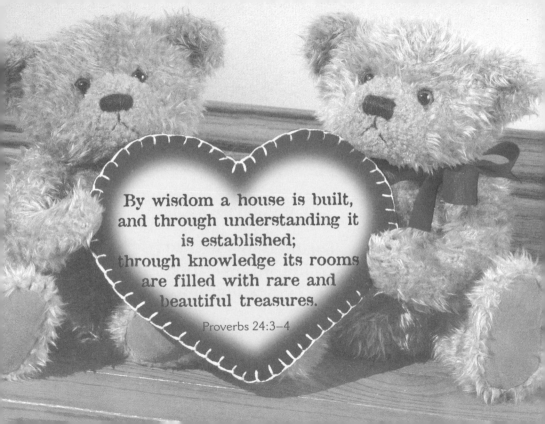

By wisdom a house is built,
and through understanding it
is established;
through knowledge its rooms
are filled with rare and
beautiful treasures.

Proverbs 24:3–4

By ourselves we can enjoy life, but to really appreciate life we must find companionship.

Glorify the LORD with me;
let us exalt his name
together.

Psalm 34:3

Friendship is to be purchased
only by friendship.

Thomas Wilson

Love and faithfulness meet together;
righteousness and peace
kiss each other.

Psalm 85:10

Friendship doubles your joys
and divides your sorrows.

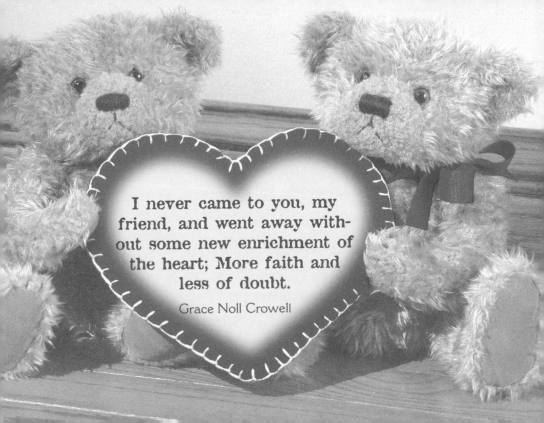

I never came to you, my
friend, and went away without some new enrichment of
the heart; More faith and
less of doubt.

Grace Noll Crowell

I will give you the...riches
stored in secret places,
so that you may know that I
am the LORD,
the God of Israel, who
summons you by name.

Isaiah 45:3

The LORD is near to all who call on him, to all who call on him in truth.

Psalm 145:18

To friendship,
every burden's light.

John Gay

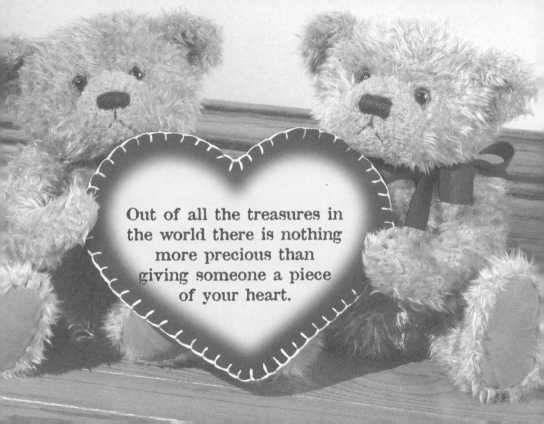

Out of all the treasures in
the world there is nothing
more precious than
giving someone a piece
of your heart.

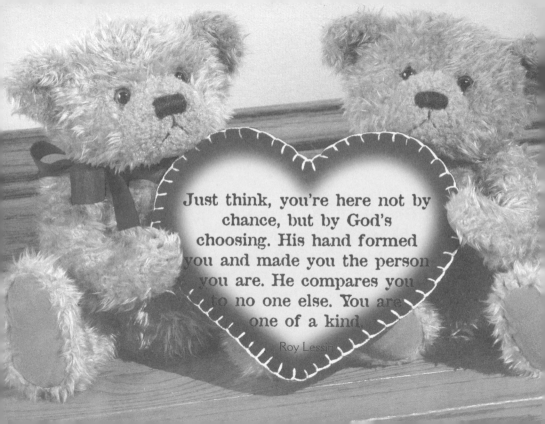

Just think, you're here not by chance, but by God's choosing. His hand formed you and made you the person you are. He compares you to no one else. You are one of a kind.

Roy Lessin

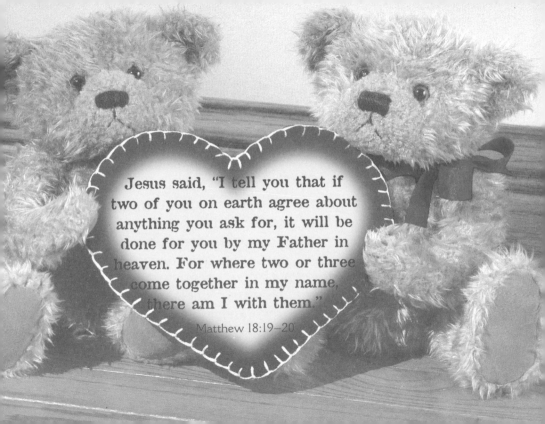

Jesus said, "I tell you that if two of you on earth agree about anything you ask for, it will be done for you by my Father in heaven. For where two or three come together in my name, there am I with them."

Matthew 18:19–20

I will always treasure our
friendship
without counting the miles
between us,
the days we've been apart,
or the differences
we share.

Where your treasure is, there your heart will be also.

Matthew 6:21

The happiness friends bring you always gives a special lift, and you realize that friendship is God's most perfect gift.

If we want a love message to be heard, it has got to be sent out. To keep a lamp burning, we have to keep putting oil in it.

Mother Teresa

I thank my God every time I remember you. In all my prayers for...you, I always pray with joy....It is right for me to feel this way about... you, since I have you in my heart.

Philippians 1:3–4, 7

Be devoted to one another in brotherly love. Honor one another above yourselves.

Romans 12:10

Those who bring sunshine to the lives of others cannot keep it from themselves.

Sir James Barrie

Love is, above all,
the gift of oneself.

Jean Anouills

Love is a fruit in season at all times, and within the reach of every hand.

Mother Teresa

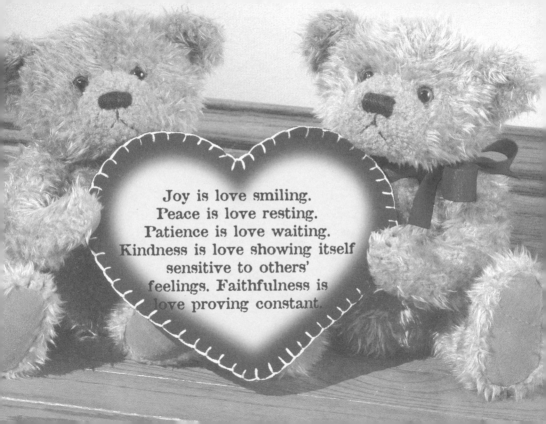

Joy is love smiling.
Peace is love resting.
Patience is love waiting.
Kindness is love showing itself
sensitive to others'
feelings. Faithfulness is
love proving constant.

The good man brings good things out of the good stored up in his heart....For out of the overflow of his heart his mouth speaks.

Luke 6:45

There is no treasure that may be compared to a faithful friend.

Roxburghe Ballads

Love is patient,
love is kind.

1 Corinthians 13:4

Caring and sharing are the
very nicest parts of love.

Roy Lessin

May happiness be thy lot,
And peace thy steps attend.
Accept the tribute of respect
From all that call thee friend.

T. W. Caldwell